Teach Me...™
Spanish
and
More Spanish

by Judy Mahoney

Teach Me Spanish and More Spanish
Two books in one, twice the fun!
36 songs to sing and learn Spanish

The classic coloring books *Teach Me Spanish* and *Teach Me More Spanish* are now combined into a new bind up edition. This new edition includes the original coloring pages from both titles with a 60 minute audio CD. *Teach Me Spanish and More Spanish* also features six new pages of expanded vocabulary and activities.

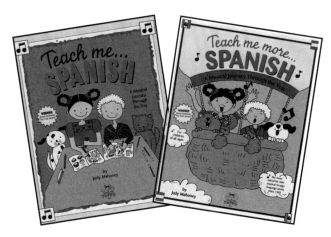

Our mission at Teach Me Tapes, Inc. is to enrich children through language learning. The ***Teach Me...*** series of books offers an engaging approach to language acquisition by using familiar children's songs and providing an audio to sing and learn. Studies show that a child's early exposure to new languages and cultures enhances learning skills and promotes a better appreciation of our multicultural world. We believe it is important for children to listen, speak, read and write the language in order to enhance the learning experience. What better gift to offer our youth than the tools and ideas to understand the world we live in?

It is interesting to note that the Spanish alphabet contains four more letters than our English alphabet. These letters are: ch, ll, ñ and rr. Also, the "k" and "w" in the Spanish alphabet are used only in words of foreign origin. Spanish nouns have a gender; therefore, the article preceding the noun indicates masculine or feminine, as well as singular or plural. Spanish-speaking countries and regions may have their own dialect or variation of the language and pronunciation.

Today's "global children" hold tomorrow's world in their hands!

Teach Me Spanish & More Spanish
Bind Up Edition
Book with CD
ISBN: 978-1-59972-602-1
Library of Congress PCN: 2009901066

Copyright © 2009 Teach Me Tapes, Inc.
6016 Blue Circle Drive
Minnetonka, MN 55343-9104
1-800-456-4656
www.teachmetapes.com

Translations are not literal.
Printed in the United States of America
10 9 8 7 6 5 4 3 2

Teach me... SPANISH

A Musical Journey Through the Day

by
Judy Mahoney

Teach Me™...
www.teachmetapes.com

 Lo Más Que Nos Reunimos

Lo más que nos reunimos, reunimos, reunimos
Lo más que nos reunimos seremos felices
Tus amigos son mis amigos y mis amigos son tus amigos
Lo más que nos reunimos seremos felices.

¡Hola! Me llamo María.
¿Cómo se llama?

Esta es mi familia.

Mi Padre

Mi Madre

Yo

Mi hermano

Mi Gato

El se llama Mishu. El es de color gris.

Mi Perro

El se llama Coloso. El es de color negro y blanco.

Esta es mi casa. Mi casa tiene un techo rojo y un jardín con las flores amarillas.

Mi cuarto es azul. Son las siete.
¡Levántate! ¡Levántate!

 Fray Felipe

Fray Felipe, Fray Felipe, ¿Duermes tú? ¿Duermes tú?
Suenan las campanas, suenan las campanas.
¡Din Dan Don!
¡Din Dan Don!

Hoy es lunes.
¿Sabes tú los días
de la semana?

LUNES

MARTES

MIÉRCOLES

JUEVES

VIERNES

SÁBADO

DOMINGO

🎵 Cabeza y Hombros Piernas y Pies

Cabeza y hombros piernas y pies piernas y pies
Cabeza y hombros piernas y pies piernas y pies
Ojos orejas boca una nariz
Cabeza y hombros piernas y pies piernas y pies.

 Está Lloviendo

Está lloviendo, está lloviendo
El viejo está roncando
Golpeó su cabeza y se fue
A la cama
No podía levantarse
En la mañana.

 Arco Iris

A veces azul, a veces verde
Los colores más lindos
Que yo he visto
Rosado y lila, amarillo–¡wii!
Me gusta sentarme en los arco iris.

Aquí está mi escuela. Yo digo, "Buenos días, Profesora".

Yo repito mis números y mi alfabeto.

María Tenía un Borreguito

María tenía un borreguito,
Borreguito, borreguito,
María tenía un borreguito
Blanco como nieve.
Un día la siguió
A la escuela, a la escuela,
A la escuela,
Un día la siguió
A la escuela,
Lo cual era prohibido.

Un Elefante

Dos elefantes fueron
A jugar
En una telaraña
Se alegraron tanto
Que llamaron
A los otros elefantes
A jugar.

Cuatro ...

La Bamba

Para bailar La Bamba
Para bailar La Bamba
Se necesita una poca
De gracia
Una poca de gracia y
Otra cosita
¡Arriba!

La Cucaracha

La Cucaracha
La Cucaracha
Ya no puede caminar
Porque no tiene
Porque le faltan
Patas para caminar.

Después de la escuela, nosotros manejamos el coche a la casa.

 Las Ruedas del Coche

Las ruedas del coche van dando vueltas,
Dando vueltas, dando vueltas,
Las ruedas del coche van dando vueltas,
Por todo el pueblo.

La bocina del coche suena pip pip pip,
Pip pip pip, pip pip pip,
La bocina del coche suena pip pip pip,
Por todo el pueblo.

Los niños en el coche dicen
"Vamos a almorzar, vamos a almorzar,
Vamos a almorzar"
Los niños en el coche dicen
Vamos a almorzar
Por todo el pueblo.

Es la hora del almuerzo.

 **Quieto Mi Niño**

Quieto mi niño no llores
Tu papá te dará unas loras
Si esas loras no cantarán
Papá te comprará una oveja
Si la oveja no da buena lana
Entonces te dará una hermana
Si tu hermana no quiere jugar
Tu papá te llevará a un lindo lugar.

Después del almuerzo tomamos una siesta.

12 DOCE

Me Gusta Ir a Pasear

Me gusta ir a pasear por la senda del cerro
Me gusta ir a pasear con mi mochila puesta atrás
Valderé, valderá, valderé, valderá, ja-ja, valderé, valderá
Con mi mochila puesta atrás.

Después de la siesta nosotros vamos al parque. Yo veo los patos. Yo canto "Me Gusta ir a Pasear" con mis amigos.

Jack y Jill

Jack y Jill subieron la cuesta
Para acarrear el agua
Jack se cayó
Quebró su corona
Y Jill se vino rodando.

Seis Patitos

Seis patitos que yo conocía
Gordos, flacos, bonitos también
Pero el patito con la pluma en su espalda
Guió a los otros con su cuac cuac cuac,
Cuac cuac cuac, cuac cuac cuac,
Guió a los otros con su cuac cuac cuac.

Yo tengo hambre. Es la hora de la comida.

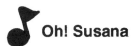 **Oh! Susana**

Yo vengo de Alabama mi banjo por mi rodilla
Me voy a Louisiana para ver a mi amor
Oh, Susana, no llores por mí
Yo vengo de Alabama mi banjo por mi rodilla.

La noche es oscura. ¿Tú ves las estrellas? Buenas noches Mamá. Buenas noches Papá. Los quiero mucho.

Buenas noches mis amigos.

 Estrellita Brillarás

Estrellita brillarás
Todo lo iluminarás
Desde aquí yo te veré
Todo el cielo azul se ve
Estrellita brillarás
Todo lo iluminarás.

El Sereno

El sereno de mi calle
Tiene una voz muy bonita
Que cuando canta las horas,
Parece una señorita
Sereno que canta, dime qué hora es
Que ha dado la una, las dos, y las tres;
Las cuatro, las cinco, las seis, las siete,
Las ocho, las nueve, las diez
Sereno que canta, dime qué hora es.

TRANSLATIONS

PAGE 1
The More We Get Together
The more we get together, together, together,
The more we get together, the happier we'll be.
For your friends are my friends
And my friends are your friends
The more we get together, the happier we'll be.

PAGE 2
Hello, my name is Marie. What is your name? This is my family. My mother, my father, my brother and me.

PAGE 3
My cat. His name is Mishu. He is grey. My dog. His name is Coloso. He is black and white. This is my house. My house has a red roof and a garden with yellow flowers.

PAGE 4
My room is blue. It is seven o'clock. Get up! Get up!

Are You Sleeping
Are you sleeping, are you sleeping?
Brother John, Brother John?
Morning bells are ringing
Morning bells are ringing
Ding, dang, dong! Ding, dang, dong!

PAGE 5
Today is Monday. Do you know the days of the week? Monday, Tuesday, Wednesday, Thursday, Friday, Saturday, Sunday.

PAGE 6
I get dressed. I put on my shirt, my pants, my shoes and my hat. I eat breakfast. I like bread and orange juice.

PAGE 7
Head, Shoulders, Knees and Toes
Head and shoulders, knees and toes, knees and toes.
Head and shoulders, knees and toes, knees and toes.
Eyes and ears and mouth and nose.
Head and shoulders, knees and toes, knees and toes.

PAGE 8
The weather is bad. It is raining. I cannot go for a walk today.

Rain, Rain, Go Away
Rain, rain, go away,
Come again another day.
Rain, rain, go away,
Little Johnny wants to play.

It's Raining, It's Pouring
It's raining, it's pouring,
The old man is snoring,
He bumped his head and went to bed
And couldn't get up in the morning.

Rainbows
Sometimes blue and sometimes green
Prettiest colors I've ever seen
Pink and purple, yellow-whee!
I love to ride those rainbows.
© Teach Me Tapes, Inc. 1985

PAGE 9
Here is my school. I say, "Good morning, Teacher." I repeat my numbers and my alphabet. One, uno; two, dos; three, tres; four, cuatro; five, cinco; six, seis; seven, siete; eight, ocho; nine, nueve; ten, diez. Yeah!
A, B, C, D, E, F, G,
H, I, J, K, L, M, N, O, P,
Q, R, S, T, U, V,
W, X, Y and Z.
Ahora sé mi abecedario. Now I know my ABCs.

PAGE 10
Mary Had a Little Lamb
Mary had a little lamb (repeat)
Its fleece was white as snow
It followed her to school one day (repeat)
Which was against the rules.

One Elephant
One elephant went out to play,
Upon a spider's web one day.
He had such enormous fun, that
He called for another elephant to come.

Two ... (repeat)
Three ... (repeat)
Four ... (repeat)
All ... (repeat)

La Bamba
To dance the bamba,
To dance the bamba,
A little grace is needed,
A little grace plus a little bit of go.

La Cucaracha
La cucaracha, la cucaracha,
Running up and down the wall
La cucaracha, la cucaracha,
Me, I have no legs at all.

PAGE 11
After school, we drive in our car to our house.

The Wheels on the Car
The wheels on the car go round and round,
Round and round, round and round,
The wheels on the car go round and round,
All around the town.

The horn on the car goes beep beep beep,
Beep beep beep, beep beep beep,
The horn on the car goes beep beep beep,
All around the town.

The children in the car say, "Let's have lunch,"
"Let's have lunch, let's have lunch,"
The children in the car say, "Let's have lunch,"
All around the town.

PAGE 12
Lunch Dialogue
Hermano: Hermana, ¿qué vamos a comer?
María: Vamos a comer tortillas con frijoles. Toma.
¿Está bien? Yo voy a probar.
Hermano: Pasa la sal.
María: Toma. Falta sal.
Hermano: Gracias.
María: ¿Quieres más frijoles?
Hermano: No, gracias.
María: Mmm ... ¡Muy ricas tortillas! ¡Gracias, Mamá!

Brother: Sister, what are we going to eat?
Marie: We're going to eat tortillas with beans. Have some. Is it OK? I'm going to try some.
Brother: Pass the salt.
Marie: Here. It's missing salt.
Brother: Thank you.
Marie: Do you want more beans?
Brother: No, thank you.
Marie: Mmm...The tortillas are very good! Thanks, Mom!

It is lunch time. After lunch, we take a nap.

Hush Little Baby
Hush little baby don't say a word,
Papa's going to buy you a mockingbird;
If that mockingbird won't sing,
Papa's going to buy you a diamond ring.
If that diamond ring turns brass,
Papa's going to buy you a looking glass;
If that looking glass falls down,
You'll still be the sweetest little baby in town.
Note: Spanish words fit music, not the English translation.

PAGE 13
After our naps, we go to the park. I see the ducks. I sing, "I Love to Go a Wandering," with my friends.

I Love to Go a Wandering
I love to go a wandering
Along the mountain path
I love to go a wandering
My knapsack on my back.
Valdore, valdora, valdore, valdora, ha-ha
Valdore, valdora
My knapsack on my back.

Jack and Jill
Jack and Jill went up the hill
To fetch a pail of water
Jack fell down and broke his crown
And Jill came tumbling after.

Six Little Ducks
Six little ducks that I once knew,
Fat ones, skinny ones, fair ones too.
But the one little duck
With the feather on his back,

He led the others with his
Quack, quack, quack,
Quack, quack, quack,
Quack, quack, quack.
He led the others with his
Quack, quack, quack.

PAGE 14
I am hungry. It is dinner time.

Oh! Susanna
Well, I come from Alabama
With a banjo on my knee,
I'm going to Louisiana, my true love for to see.
Oh, Susanna, won't you cry for me.
'Cause I come from Alabama
With a banjo on my knee.

PAGE 15
The night is dark. Do you see the stars?

Twinkle, Twinkle
Twinkle, twinkle, little star,
How I wonder what you are.
Up above the world so high,
Like a diamond in the sky,
Twinkle, twinkle, little star,
How I wonder what you are!

El Sereno
The night watchman of my street
Has a very nice voice
When he sings the hours
He sounds like a woman.
Night watchman that sings
Tell me what time it is
He has announced one o'clock
Two, three, four, five, six, seven,
Eight, nine, ten.
Night watchman who sings
Tell me what time it is.

PAGE 15
Good night, Mommy. Good night, Daddy. I love you.

Good Night, My Friends
Good night, my friends, good night
Good night, my friends, good night
Good night, my friends,
Good night, my friends,
Good night, my friends, good night

Good night!

Note: The Spanish language respects the content of the English traditional songs, therefore, this is not a word-for-word literal translation due to the different structure of the languages.

Teach me more... SPANISH

by
Judy Mahoney

A Musical Journey Through the Year

Learn Spanish the fun way!

Teach Me...™
www.teachmetapes.com

María: Hola. Mi nombre es María. Este es mi hermano. Su nombre es Pedro. Tenemos un perro. Su nombre es Coloso. Tenemos un gato. Su nombre es Michín. Síguenos durante el año.

Tú Cantarás y Yo Cantaré

Tú cantarás y yo cantaré y todos juntos cantaremos
Tú cantarás y yo cantaré con frío o con calor.

Words and music by Ella Jenkins, ASCAP. Copyright 1966. Ell-Bern Publishing Co.

Pedro: Es primavera. Yo siembro una flor en el jardín. Mira mis rosas rojas y amarillas.

María: Yo siembro semillas de verduras en mi huerta. Este año cosecharé tomates, pimientos verdes y zanahorias.

Avena, Fréjol, y Cebada Se Cultiva

Avena, fréjol, y cebada se cultiva, *(repeat)*
¿Sabes tú o yo o cualquiera
Cómo avena, fréjol y cebada se cultiva?

María: Hoy vamos al zoológico. Mira el león, la jirafa y el simio.
Pedro: Mi animal favorito en el zoológico es el cocodrilo.

Vamos al Zoológico

Vamos con mamá al zoológico mañana
Zoológico mañana, zoológico mañana
(repita)
Todo el día
Vamos al zoológico
Vienes tú también *(repita)*
Todos vamos al zoológico.

Mira a los simios
Colgando de las ramas *(repita)*
Todo el día.

Mira a los lagartos
Nadando en el agua *(repita)*
Todo el día.

Tingaleo

Tingaleo, ven borriquito ven
Tingaleo, ven borriquito ven
Burrito veloz y lento también
Mi burro viene y mi burro va
Burrito veloz y lento también
Mi burro viene y mi burro va.

María: Mi cumpleaños es el 10 de mayo. Tendré una fiesta con mis amigos. Mi mamá me hará una torta grande y redonda.

Pedro: Bueno. Vamos a jugar a Simón Dice.

María: A mis amigos y a mí nos gusta romper la piñata.

El Juego de Simón Dice

Simón dice ... "lleva la mano derecha a la cabeza."
... "toca el suelo."
... "zapatea."
... "aplaude."
... "di tu nombre."

Pedro: Después de la primavera viene el verano. En el verano vamos a la playa. Llevo mi balón de playa y mi barco de juguete.

María: Yo llevo mi cubo y mi pala a la playa. Nos ponemos el vestido de baño y construimos muchos castillos gigantescos en la arena. ¡Coloso, no lo derribes!

Rema, Rema, Rema

Rema, rema, rema tu bote
Suave sobre el río
Alegremente, alegremente,
La vida es un sueño.

5 CINCO

María: Después de nadar, tomamos el almuerzo.
Comemos pan, queso y fruta. Es delicioso.
Pedro: ¡Oh, no! ¡Mira las hormigas!
María: después del día de campo, nos vamos a dar una caminata.

Día

Día, es de día, viene la mañana y me quiero ir *(repita)*
Trabajo por la noche hasta la mañana, viene la mañana y me quiero ir
Apilo bananas hasta la mañana, viene la mañana y me quiero ir.
Ven contador y cuenta las bananas, viene... *(repita)*
Levanta seis, siete, ocho racimos, viene... *(repita)*
(Coro)
Un racimo hermoso de bananas maduras, viene... *(repita)*

MES DE AGOSTO

TRICERATOPE

María: Hoy vamos al museo de historia natural.
Pedro: Es mi lugar favorito porque hay dinosaurios.
Mira el triceratope. Tiene tres cuernos en la cabeza.

7 SIETE

María: Luego cruzamos la calle para visitar el museo de arte.
Pedro: Me gusta mirar los toros en las pinturas de Goya. Me imagino que yo soy el torero.

Chica Canela en la Plaza

Chica canela en la plaza,
Tra-la-la-la-la *(repita)*
Parece azúcar
Y ciruela.

2. Qué bien te mueves...
3. Salta sobre la mar...
4. Haz la locomoción...

María: Después del verano viene el otoño. Las hojas se vuelven doradas, rojas y moradas. Yo estoy recogiendo las hojas y las avellanas.

De Colores

De colores, de colores se visten los campos en la primavera.
De colores, de colores son los pajaritos que vienen de afuera.
De colores, de colores es el arco iris que vemos lucir.
Y por eso los grandes amores de muchos colores me gustan a mí.

Pedro: Antes de volver a la escuela visitamos la finca de mi abuelo. Les damos comida a las vacas, a las gallinas y a los cerdos.

María: Abuelo toma la lana de las ovejas. Después nos lleva a pasear con nuestros primos.

Ovejita Negra

Ovejita negra, tienes mucha lana
Sí señor, sí señor, tres canastas llenas
Una para mi maestro y una para mi dama
Una para el niño que vive más allá
Ovejita negra, tienes mucha lana
Sí señor, sí señor, tres canastas llenas.

A la Finca de Mi Abuelo

Ya nos vamos, ya nos vamos
A la finca de mi abuelo *(repita)*
Una vaca parda en la finca
De mi abuelo *(repita)*
La vaca, la vaca hace mu. *(repita)*

...Una gallina roja. *(Clo, clo)*

El Señor MacDonald

Señor MacDonald tenía una finca, E I E I O
Y en su granja había una vaca, E I E I O
Con mu aquí, y mu allá
Aquí un mu, allá un mu
En todas partes mu, mu
Señor MacDonald tenía una finca, E I E I O

...tenía un pollo, gato, oveja.

María: Hoy nuestros padres nos llevan a la feria de la cosecha. Los agricultores traen sus viandas y sus animales para que sean juzgados.

Pedro: Hay muchas máquinas para los niños. A mí me gustan los caballitos.

11 ONCE

Pedro: Es el Día de Todos los Santos. Estoy tallando una cara en mi calabaza.

María: Esta noche me pondré mi disfraz de Caperucita Roja y Coloso será el lobo. Pedro será un vaquero. Después iremos a pedir golosinas con nuestros amigos.

Cinco Calabazas

Cinco calabazas sentadas en un banco
La primera dijo, "Se está haciendo tarde."
La segunda dijo, "Hay brujas en el aire."
Dijo la tercera, "No nos importa."
La cuarta dijo, "Echemos a correr."
La quinta dijo, "Yo quiero divertirme."
"Uu-uu," dijo el viento, y la luz se apagó
Y las cinco calabazas comenzaron a rodar.

Pedro: Mira, la nieve está cayendo. Vamos a jugar en la nieve. Llevamos nuestros trineos y nos deslizamos por la cuesta.

María: Después hacemos un muñeco de nieve. Con ojos de carbón, nariz de zanahoria y brazos de ramas. Lleva puesta la bufanda de mi mamá.

Un Muñeco de Nieve

Hay un amigo mío
Lo conoces también
Lleva un sombrero
Es muy chévere

Tiene ojos negros
Nariz de zanahoria
Dos brazos de palitos
Y un abrigo blanco

¿Adivinaste el nombre?
O ¿necesitas algo más?
¡Nunca verás su cara
En otra estación!
¿Quién es?

¡Adivinen quién es!
¿Quién es?
¡Es un muñeco de nieve!

Noche de Paz

Noche de paz, noche de amor
Todos duermen alrededor
Todos sueñan en la obscuridad
Armonías de felicidad
Armonías de paz
Armonías de paz.

FELIZ AÑO NUEVO

María: Es la época de fiestas. Nosotros celebramos la Navidad. Hacemos galletas y decoramos nuestra casa. Cantamos canciones especiales.

Pedro: El primero de enero comienza un año nuevo. Tendremos una fiesta para despedir al Año Viejo y recibir el Año Nuevo.

MES DE FEBRERO

María: En febrero celebramos el carnaval de Mardi Gras. Es divertido coger las golosinas en el desfile. Cantamos y bailamos con nuestros amigos. Ahora sabemos los meses del año. ¿Y tú? Enero, febrero, marzo, abril, mayo, junio, julio, agosto, septiembre, octubre, noviembre, diciembre. Adiós queridos amigos.

15 QUINCE

TRANSLATIONS

PAGE 1
You'll Sing a Song
You'll sing a song and I'll sing a song
And we'll sing a song together.
You'll sing a song and I'll sing a song,
In warm or wintry weather.

MARIE: Hello. My name is Marie. This is my brother. His name is Peter. We have a dog. His name is Coloso. We have a cat. His name is Michin. Follow us through the year.

PAGE 2 MARCH
PETER: It is spring. I plant a flower in the garden. Look at my red and yellow roses.
MARIE: I plant vegetable seeds in my garden. This year I will grow tomatoes, peppers and carrots.

Oats and Beans and Barley
Oats and beans and barley grow. *(repeat)*
Do you or I or anyone know
How oats and beans and barley grow?

PAGE 3 APRIL
MARIE: Today we go to the zoo. Look at the lion, the giraffe and the monkey.
PETER: My favorite animal at the zoo is the crocodile.

Going to the Zoo
Mommy's taking us to the zoo tomorrow,
Zoo tomorrow, zoo tomorrow
Mommy's taking us to the zoo tomorrow,
We can stay all day.
We're going to the zoo, zoo, zoo.
How about you, you, you?
You can come too, too, too
We're going to the zoo, zoo, zoo.

2. Look at all the monkeys swinging in the trees...
3. Look at all the crocodiles swimming in the water...

Tingalayo
Tingalayo, come little donkey come. *(repeat)*
Me donkey fast, me donkey slow,
Me donkey come and me donkey go.
Me donkey fast, me donkey slow,
Me donkey come and me donkey go.

Tingalayo, come little donkey come. *(repeat)*
Me donkey he, me donkey haw,
Me donkey sleep in a bed of straw.
Me donkey dance, me donkey sing,
Me donkey wearing a diamond ring.

PAGE 4 MAY
Que Los Cumplas Feliz
Que los cumplas feliz *(repeat 3 times)*

Happy Birthday to You
Happy birthday to you! *(repeat 3 times)*

MARIE: My birthday is May 10. I will have a party with my friends. My mother will bake me a big, round cake.
PETER: OK. Let's play "Simon Says."

Simon Says Game
Simon says ... "put your right hand on your head"
... "touch the ground"
... "tap your foot"
... "clap your hands"
... "say your name"
MARIE: My friends and I like to break the piñata.

PAGE 5 JUNE
PETER: After spring, it is summer. In the summer, we go to the beach. I bring my beach ball and toy boat.
MARIE: I bring my sand pail and shovel to the beach. We put on our swimsuits and build huge castles in the sand. Coloso, don't knock it down!

Row, Row, Row Your Boat
Row, row, row your boat
Gently down the stream
Merrily, merrily, merrily, merrily
Life is but a dream.

PAGE 6 JULY
MARIE: After we swim, we eat our picnic lunch. We eat bread, cheese and fruit. It is delicious.
PETER: Oh no! Look at the ants!
MARIE: After our picnic, we go for a walk.

Day-O
Chorus: Day-o, me say day-o
    Daylight come and me wan' go home (repeat)
Work all night 'til the mornin' come,
    Daylight come and me wan' go home
Stack banana 'til the mornin' come,
    Daylight come and me wan' go home
Come mister tallyman, tally me banana,
    Daylight come and me wan' go home *(repeat)*
Lift six hand, seven hand, eight hand bunch.
    Daylight come and me wan' go home *(repeat)*
Chorus
A beautiful bunch of ripe banana,
    Daylight come and me wan' go home *(repeat)*
Lift six hand, seven hand, eight hand bunch.
    Daylight come and me wan' go home *(repeat)*
Chorus
Come mister tallyman, tally me banana,
    Daylight come and me wan' go home *(repeat)*
Chorus

PAGE 7 AUGUST
MARIA: Today we go to the natural history museum.
PETER: It is my favorite place because there are so many dinosaurs. Look at the triceratops. It has three horns on its head.

PAGE 8 AUGUST
MARIE: Next, we go across the street to visit the art museum.
PETER: I like to look at the bulls in Goya's paintings. I pretend I am the matador.

Brown Girl in the Ring
Brown girl in the ring,
Tra-la-la-la-la *(repeat)*
She looks like a sugar
And a plum, plum, plum.

2. Show me a motion...
3. Skip across the ocean...
4. Do the locomotion...

PAGE 9 SEPTEMBER

MARIE: After summer, it is autumn. The leaves turn gold, red and purple. I am gathering leaves and hazelnuts.

De Colores
Colors...in many colors
The fields dress themselves in springtime;
Colors...of many colors
Are the birds all around us;
Colors...of many colors
Is the rainbow we see shining;
And this is why the many colors of love
Are pleasing to me.

PAGE 10 OCTOBER

PETER: Before we go back to school, we visit Grandpa's farm. We feed the cows, chickens and pigs.
MARIE: Grandpa shears the wool from the sheep. Later, he takes us on a hayride with our cousins.

Down on Grandpa's Farm
Oh, we're on our way, we're on our way
On our way to Grandpa's farm *(repeat)*
Down on Grandpa's farm there is a big brown cow *(repeat)*
The cow, she makes a sound like this: Moo!
2. ... there is a little red hen *(repeat)*
   The hen, she makes a sound like this: Cluck! Cluck!

Baa Baa Black Sheep
Baa baa black sheep, have you any wool?
Yes sir, yes sir, three bags full.
One for my master and
One for my dame,
One for the little boy who lives down the lane.
Baa baa black sheep, have you any wool?
Yes sir, yes sir, three bags full.

Old MacDonald
Old MacDonald had a farm, E I E I O
And on his farm he had a cow, E I E I O
With a moo, moo here and a moo, moo there
Here a moo, there a moo, everywhere a moo, moo
Old Mac Donald had a farm, E I E I O.
...had a chicken, cat, sheep!

PAGE 11 OCTOBER

MARIE: Today our parents take us to the harvest fair. The farmers bring their vegetables and animals to be judged.
PETER: There are many rides for the children. I love to ride the merry-go-round.

PAGE 12 OCTOBER/NOVEMBER

PETER: It is All Saint's Day*. I am carving a face on my pumpkin.
MARIE: Tonight I will dress up in my Little Red Riding Hood costume and Coloso will be the wolf. Peter will be a cowboy. Then we will go trick or treating with our friends.

Five Little Pumpkins
Five little pumpkins sitting on a gate
The first one said, "Oh my, it's getting late."
The second one said, "There are witches in the air."
The third one said, "But we don't care."
The fourth one said, "Let's run and run and run."
The fifth one said, "I'm ready for some fun."

*Corresponds to Halloween in the United States.

"Oo-oo," went the wind, and out went the light,
And the five little pumpkins rolled out of sight.

PAGE 13 DECEMBER

PETER: Look, snow is falling. Let's go and play in the snow. We take our sleds and slide down the hill.
MARIE: Then we build a snowman. He has coal eyes, a carrot nose and stick arms. He wears my mother's scarf.

Silent Night
Silent night, holy night,
All is calm, all is bright.
'Round yon Virgin, Mother and Child,
Holy infant so tender and mild,
Sleep in heavenly peace. *(repeat)*

Snowman Song
There's a friend of mine
You might know him, too
Wears a derby hat
He's real cool.

He has coal black eyes
An orangy carrot nose
Two funny stick-like arms
And a snowy overcoat.

Have you guessed his name
Or do you need a clue?
You'll never see his face
In autumn, summer, spring.

PAGE 14 DECEMBER/JANUARY

MARIE: It is holiday time. We celebrate Christmas. We bake cookies and decorate our house. We sing special songs.
PETER: January first begins the new year. We have a party to say good-bye to the old year and welcome the new year.

La Raspa
This is fun, traditional dance music.

PAGE 15 FEBRUARY

MARIE: In February, we celebrate the Mardi Gras carnival. It is fun. I like to catch candy at the parade. We sing and dance with our friends.
PETER: Now we know the months of the year. Do you?

JANUARY, FEBRUARY, MARCH, APRIL, MAY, JUNE, JULY, AUGUST, SEPTEMBER, OCTOBER, NOVEMBER, DECEMBER.

Good-bye, dear friends!
Note: The Spanish language respects the content of the English traditional songs, therefore, this is not a word-for-word literal translation due to the different structure of the languages.

NOTES

APPENDIX:
HOW TO PRONOUNCE THE SPANISH ALPHABET

The Alphabet (El Alfabeto)

a	ah	ñ	eñe (pronounce enye)
b	be	o	o
c	ce	p	pe
ch	che	q	cu
d	de	r	ere
e	eh	rr	erre
f	efe	s	ese
g	ge	t	te
h	hache (h is silent in Spanish)	u	oo
i	ee	v	uve
j	jota	w	doble v (w only in foreign-origin words)
k	ca (k only in foreign-origin words)		
l	ele	x	equis
ll	elle (pronounce elye)	y	i griega
m	eme	z	zeta
n	ene		

PRONUNCIATION KEY FOR SPANISH

Vowels (Las Vocales)

a   ah, as in "father" (casa, más, amigo)

e   a, as in "may" (Pedro, mesa, madre)

i   e, as in "see" (mi, María, día)

o   o, as in "hope" (con, tomo, los)

u   oo, as in "boo!" (jugo, gusta, lunes)
-When ue or ui combinations are used following g or q, don't pronounce the u. Q will have the k sound (que, aquí, queso), and the g will be hard (guitarra, guía, guerra).

y   e, as in "see"
-When used as a vowel at the end of a word, or when used alone (y, hoy, hay).

PRONUNCIATION KEY FOR SPANISH

Consonants (Las Consonantes)

b   b (bueno)
c   When found before e or i, c is pronounced like s in American Spanish, but like th in Castilian Spanish (felices, gracias). When found before other letters, pronounced like k (como).
ch ch (chaqueta)
d   th, as in they (put tongue between teeth) (día)
f   f (familia)
g   When found before e or i, g is pronounced like a guttural h (gente). In other circumstances, pronounced like hard g (gris).
h   silent (hoy)
j   guttural h (jugo)
k   k (used only in words of foreign origin)
l   l (lunes)
ll In American Spanish, pronounced as y, as in yes; in Castilian Spanish, pronounced as lli, as in million (llama).
m   m (mi)
n   n (no)
ñ   ny, as in canyon (niña)
p   p (padre)
q   k (que)
r   While pronouncing an English r, tongue should bounce off the roof of your mouth (mira). When a word begins with r, the r can be pronounced more like the rr (rojo) (see below).
rr Like r, above, but with two or three bounces of tongue off roof of mouth (perro).
s   s (siete)
t   Pronounce between an English t and d, placing tip of tongue behind the upper teeth (techo).
v   b (vamos)
w   w (used only in words of foreign origin)
x   In American Spanish, with very few exceptions (in words like México, Ximena and Texas, the x is pronounced like the Spanish j), the x is like the English x. In Castilian Spanish, when x appears before a consonant, it is usually pronounced like s (exacto, extra).
y   y as in yes, when used as a consonant (yo)
z   s, in American Spanish; but th, in Castilian Spanish (zapato)

The letter b, d, f, k, l, m, n, p, q and v have the same sound as English.
H is usually silent and w is pronounced as v.

El Alfabeto Español

A B C CH D E F G H I J K L LL LL M N Ñ O P Q R RR S T U V W X Y Z

el arco iris

la boca

el coche

la chaqueta

el dinosaurio

las estrellas

las flores

el gato

los hombros

el invierno

el jardín

el koala

rainbow · mouth · ear · jacket · dinosaur · stars · flowers · cat · shoulders · winter · garden · koala

el león

la lluvia

las marionetas

la nariz

el ñandú

el oso de peluche

el perro

el queso

el reloj

el borreguito

el sombrero

la taza

uno

el vaso

w

el xilófono

yo

los zapatos

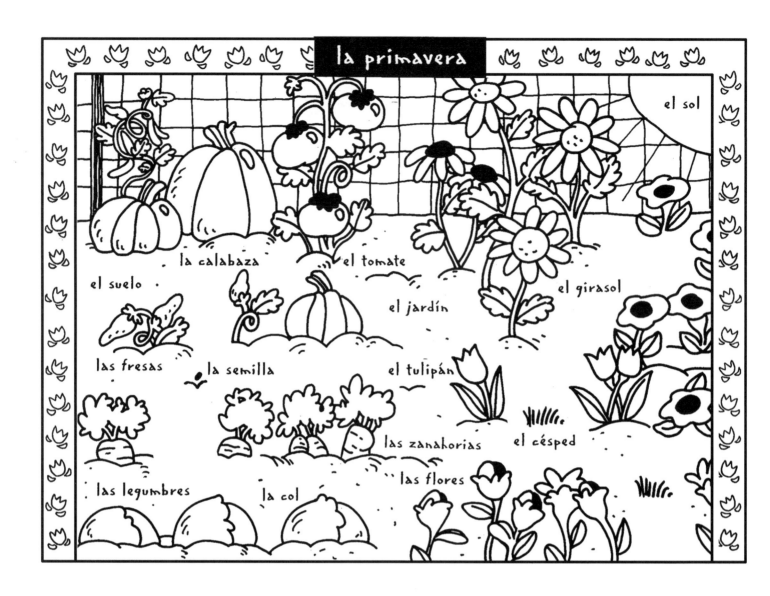

Vocabulario del primavera
Spring Vocabulary
Find the matching words in the picture.

soil _____   garden _____

strawberries _____   tulip _____

vegetables _____   carrots _____

pumpkin _____   flowers _____

seed _____   sunflower _____

cabbage _____   grass _____

tomato _____   sun _____

las nubes

las gafas

la mariposa

el vestido de baño

el barco de vela

el lago

las olas

la camiseta

la playa

el queso

la hormiga

el termos

la arena

la taza

la banana

el picnic

la cobija

los zapatos

Vocabulario del verano
Summer Vocabulary
Find the matching words in the picture.

clouds _____	cup _____
lake _____	thermos _____
beach _____	glasses _____
ant _____	swimsuit _____
sand _____	shirt _____
blanket _____	cheese _____
butterfly _____	banana _____
sailboat _____	picnic _____
waves _____	shoes _____

Vocabulario del otoño
Autumn Vocabulary
Find the matching words in the picture.

sky _____

dog _____

leaves _____

apples _____

sweater _____

coat _____

cat _____

basket _____

skirt _____

pants _____

bird _____

tree _____

chestnuts _____

rake _____

Vocabulario del invierno
Winter Vocabulary
Find the matching words in the picture.

hill _____

jacket _____

ice _____

snowflake _____

boots _____

cap _____

overcoat _____

sled _____

scarf _____

gloves _____

skates _____

snow _____

hat _____

eyes of coal _____

carrot _____

stick _____

snowman _____

ANSWER KEY FOR SEASONS VOCABULARY WORDS

La primavera (Spring)

el suelo	soil	el jardín	garden
las fresas	strawberries	el tulipán	tulip
las legumbres	vegetables	las zanahorias	carrots
la calabaza	pumpkin	las flores	flowers
la semilla	seed	el girasol	sunflower
la col	cabbage	el césped	grass
el tomate	tomato	el sol	sun

El verano (Summer)

las nubes	clouds	la taza	cup
el lago	lake	el termos	thermos
la playa	beach	las gafas	glasses
la hormiga	ant	el vestido de baño	swimsuit
la arena	sand	la camiseta	shirt
la cobija	blanket	el queso	cheese
la mariposa	butterfly	la banana	banana
el barco de vela	sailboat	el picnic	picnic
las olas	waves	los zapatos	shoes

El otoño (Autumn)

el cielo	sky	el perro	dog
las hojas	leaves	las manzanas	apples
el suéter	sweater	el saco	coat
el gato	cat	la canasta	basket
la falda	skirt	los pantalones	pants
el pájaro	bird	el árbol	tree
las castañas	chestnuts	el rastrillo	rake

El invierno (Winter)

la cuesta	hill	los guantes	gloves
la chaqueta	jacket	los patines	skates
el hielo	ice	la nieve	snow
el copo de nieve	snowflake	el sombrero	hat
las botas	boots	los ojos de carbón	eyes of coal
la gorra	cap	la zanahoria	carrot
el abrigo	overcoat	el palo	stick
el trineo	sled	el muñeco de nieve	snowman
la bufanda	scarf		